There once was a **LLAMA** who always stirred up **DRAMA!**

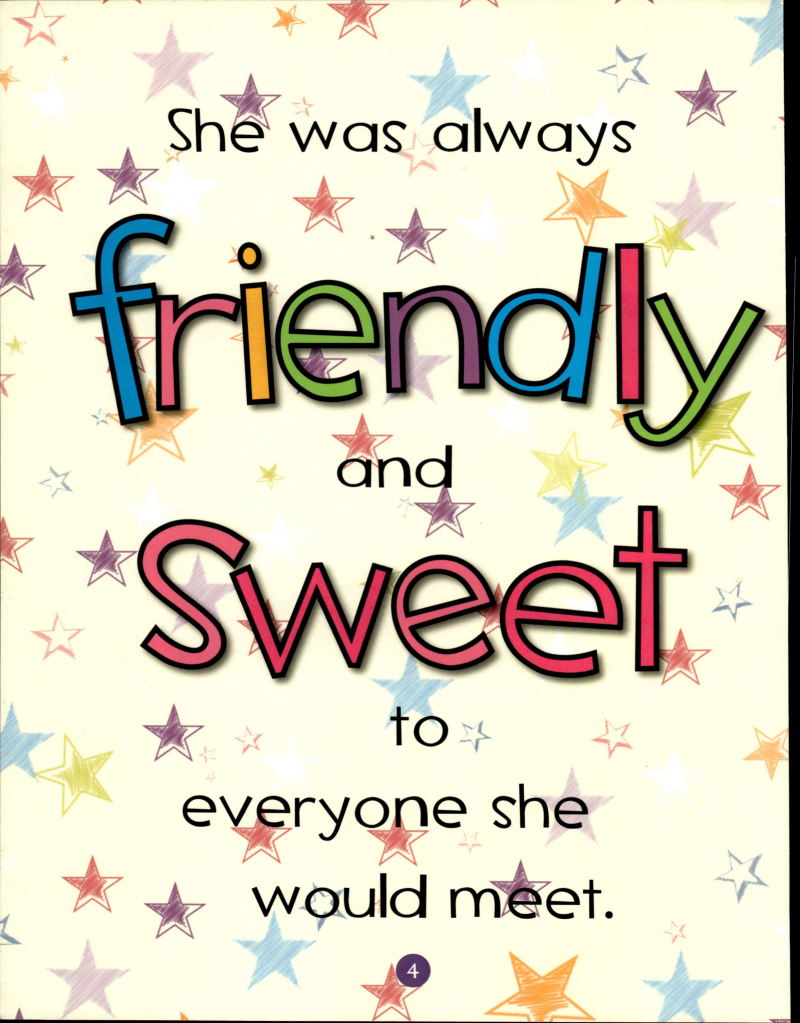

© 2024, 2018, 2014, 2013, 2012 by YouthLight
Chapin, SC 29036

All rights reserved. No part of this book may be reproduced or transmitted in any form or by any means, electronic, mechanical, including photocopying, recording, or by any information storage and retrieval system, except in the case of reviews, without the express written permission of the publisher, except where permitted by law.

Written by: Susan Bowman
Illustrations by: Poppy Moon

ISBN: 978-1-59850-120-9

Library of Congress Control Number: 2012936626

Printed in the United States
10 9 8 7 6 5

YOUTHLIGHT

PO Box 115 • Chapin, SC 29036
(803) 345-1070

www.youthlight.com

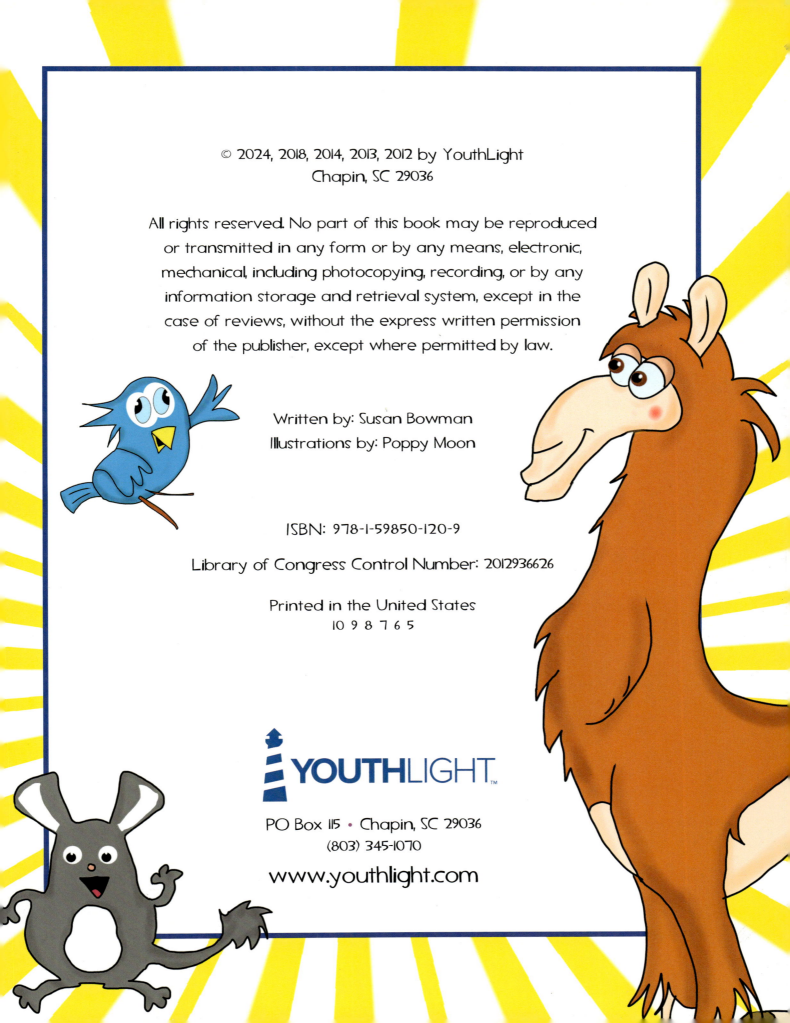

This book is dedicated to all the students who speak up when they see other students being bullied and refuse to be part of gossip and rumors. By intervening on other's behalf you are role modeling what all children need to do to put an end to gossiping, rumoring and ultimately, bullying. You can make the difference!

She **always** wanted to get the **attention** of the other animals.

It didn't matter what they were doing

she would always join in.

If they shared anything private with her, she would........

She would get all the other llamas, chinchillas, and condors

ALL

STIRRED UP!

Because some of what she said

WAS TRUE

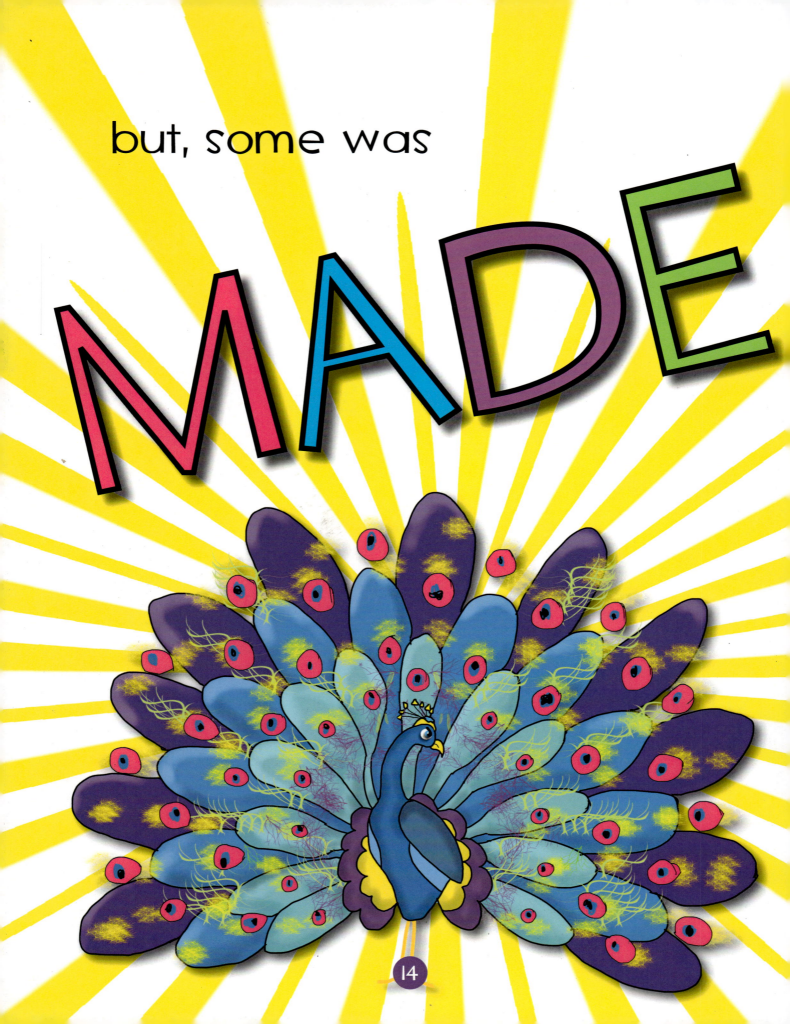

She thought that by adding the others into the DRAMA it made it more EXCiTiNG!

Then everyone was UPSET and blamed the other for what they heard.

The other animals soon learned who started the rumors and did not want to tell the Drama Llama

ANYTHING!

GOOD or BAD!

She noticed no one wanted to talk to her and she became

Lonely and Sad.

She found herself all alone during recess and at lunch.

After awhile the other animals noticed her

all alone

and decided to ask her,

"why do you like to STIR UP DRAMA LLAMA?" so much

The llama said,

"I thought you wouldn't like me if I was boring and ordinary."

The other animals laughed and told her she did not have to be popular to be their friend.

That being genuine and kind, and not spreading rumors can make this all end.

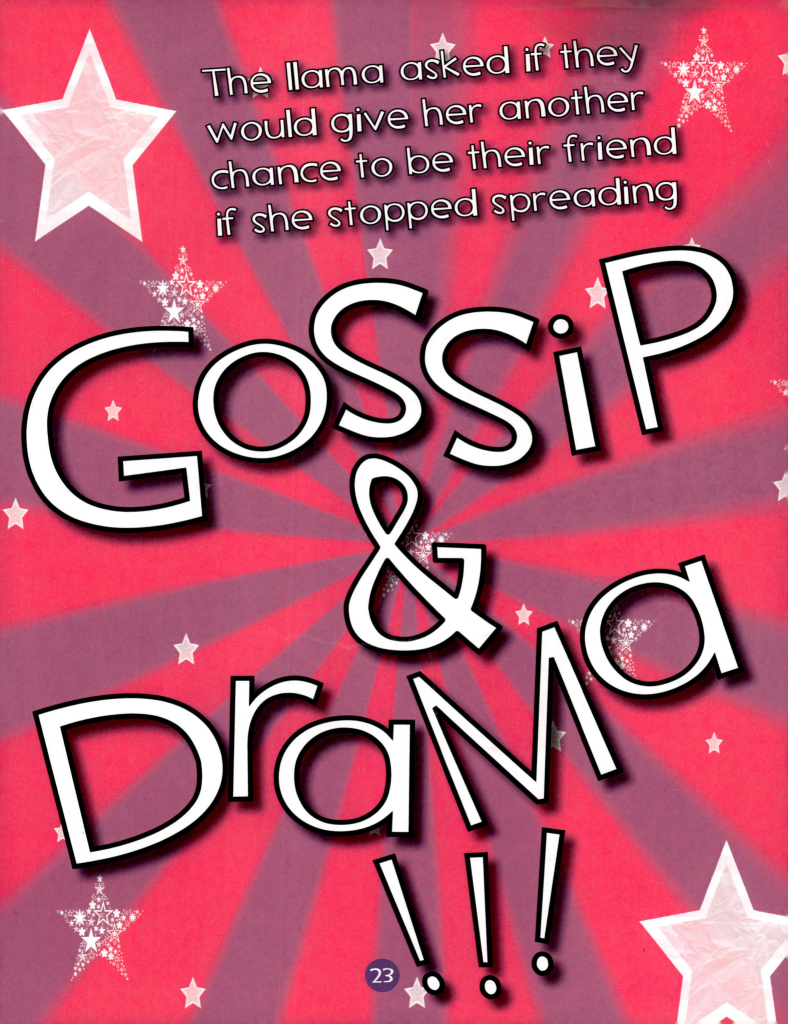

The owl said, "If you are going to talk about others when they are not around

REMEMBER...

"Rumors Hurt and cause others to Go Away

But Nice Words Make others Want to Stay."

The animals all welcomed her to join them and said to her,

"We don't even know your real name!"

The llama told them her real name was,

"Lucy"

and they all decided to play a fun game!

"Rumors Hurt and cause others to Go Away

But Nice Words Make others Want to Stay."

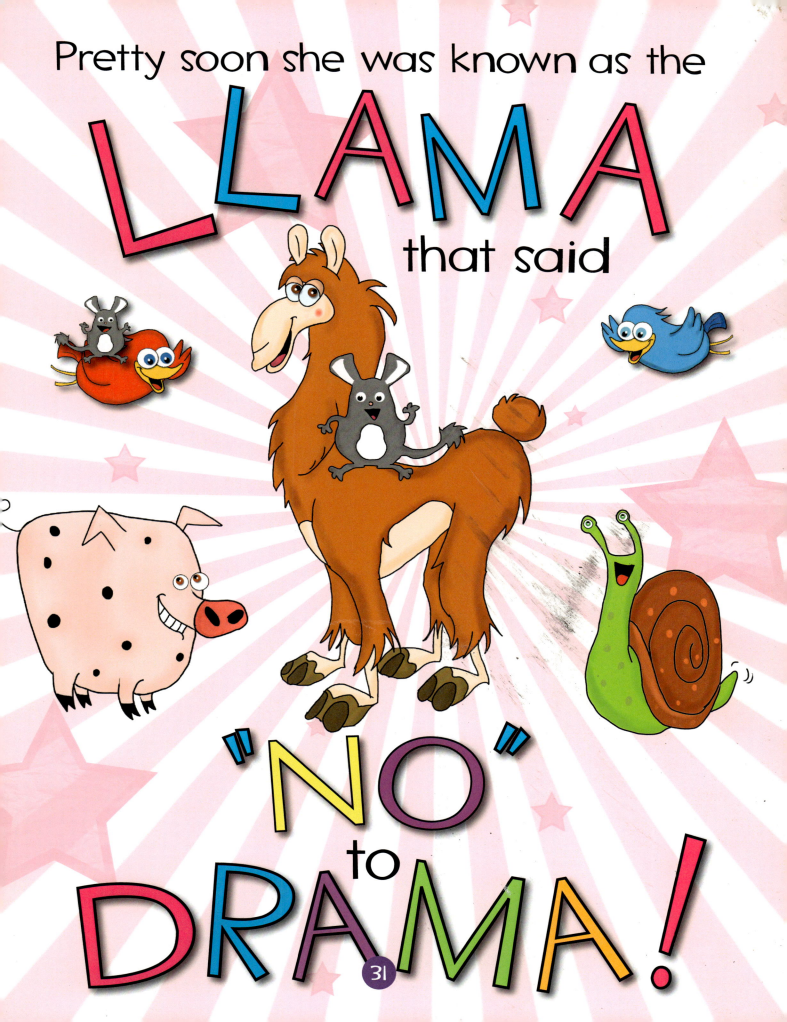

About the Author

Susan Bowman is a former high school counselor and Licensed Professional counselor. She has presented workshops and conference keynotes on the topic of girl bullying, self-injury and other issues related to girl's self-esteem. She also raised three daughters as a single parent mom. With all her experience working with young girls she has seen how drama can negatively affect relationships and hurt reputations.

Susan has written numerous other books including her own memoir. You can find her books at www.youthlight.com.

About the Illustrator

Dr. Poppy Moon, a National Board Certified Licensed Professional Counselor, works as an elementary school counselor and in private practice. She is a self-taught artist and enjoys using creativity in her work with kids. Dr. Moon lives in Tuscaloosa, Alabama with a menagerie of quirky animals.